Quilting **A**ctivities
Across the Curriculum

A Thematic Unit Filled With Activities Linked to
Math, Language Arts, Social Studies, and Science

by Wendy Buchberg

SCHOLASTIC
PROFESSIONAL BOOKS

NEW YORK ◆ TORONTO ◆ LONDON ◆ AUCKLAND ◆ SYDNEY

Dedication
To Annie, Meredith, and Alan,
the connecting threads
in the patchwork of my life.

Acknowledgments

Although I am not a highly skilled quilter myself, my love of the craft and appreciation of its history and beauty led me to share my passion with my first-grade students at South Hill Elementary School in Ithaca, New York. The unexpected result was much like the making of a patchwork quilt itself. Children of diverse backgrounds were excited to find threads of common interest as we fit into place intriguing learning connections—pattern and color, geometry and math, literature and writing, history and science—all inspired by quilts! It was the children's enthusiasm and inquisitiveness that inspired me to create this book.

I owe a debt of gratitude to Sandy Rouleau, my dear friend and colleague, who spent countless hours with me planning, researching, and co-teaching the quilting unit and helping to put together the magnificent quilts our first-grade classes designed. Karen Krupnick, Monica Edinger, and Martha Obrycki all inspired me to develop the unit into book form.

My sincere appreciation goes to the students of Ellen Rowe, Margaret Hornbrook, and Sharon Ossont at Fall Creek Elementary School in Ithaca, New York, for graciously allowing me to photograph them in action during their quilting activities and for sharing their beautiful paper patterns with me. I'm also grateful to Mitch Weiss and Martha Hamilton, the "Beauty and the Beast" Storytellers, who researched and helped me locate some wonderful folk tales about quilts. Melanie Walker of Caroline Elementary School in Ithaca, New York, and Will Edmondson, my former first-grade student, entrusted me with wonderful student-made quilts to photograph for this book.

Terry Cooper, Liza Charlesworth, and Joan Novelli of Scholastic Professional Books and Adrienne Schure of Scholastic Network were instrumental in bringing this project to fruition. My sincere thanks go out to them for the doors they opened for me.

Finally, I offer a special thank-you to my parents and family for the support they have given me as a teacher, writer, and quilt admirer.

Cover design by Jaime Lucero and Vincent Ceci

Interior design by Ellen Matlach Hassell for Boultinghouse & Boultinghouse, Inc.

Interior Illustrations by Maxie Chambliss and Ellen Matlach Hassell

Photos courtesy of the author.

ISBN 0-590-96558 -1

Copyright © 1996 by Wendy Buchberg

All rights reserved. Printed in the U.S.A.

12 11 10 9 8 7 6 5 4   8 9/9/01/0

Contents

continued on the next page

A Note From the Author

Not long ago, I was preparing to introduce patterns to my first-grade students. Although patterning was part of our math lessons, I wanted to integrate patterns into our reading and writing workshops and other areas of the curriculum. While struggling to find a thematic umbrella to unify these curricular strands, I happened to share with my class a shoebox full of sampler quilt blocks that had been tucked away in my closet. I had made them several years ago while taking an adult education class but hadn't found time to complete the quilt. I had an inkling that the children might be intrigued as I explained the names of the different patterns on the blocks, but I was overwhelmed by the explosion of insightful questions and excited comments that burst forth as they passed around the fabric blocks and examined them closely.

"This one's made of all triangles, but some of the triangles make squares!"

"I wonder how many pieces you sewed together to make this block.... Let's count!"

"This one's called Churn Dash. What's a churn, and what's a dash?"

"Are there enough blocks to make a quilt here? Let's see... if we put four blocks in a row, how many rows can we make?"

One thing led to another, and before I knew it, my class had shown me the direction our integrated study of patterns would take. We were studying quilts! This is how our journey into classroom quilting began, and now it has become one of my favorite units to teach. After discovering the wealth of teaching and project ideas extending into every area of the curriculum, you may be hooked, too!

—Wendy Buchberg

Above: The author quilting with her daughter

Using This Book

How can something as warm, soft, and gentle as a patchwork quilt possibly be the thematic focus of a teaching unit? Here are just a few of the ways you can use this book to make connections across your curriculum.

Math

Quilting lends itself to all kinds of fascinating hands-on geometry and mathematics applications, using basic supplies and manipulatives you may already have in your classroom. For a collection of quilting projects that make math connections, see page 24. The culminating project outlined on pages 51–56 invites children to apply what they've learned as they design patterned quilt blocks for a class quilt. (Like the other activities in this book, you can choose from paper or fabric.)

Language Arts

The wealth of quality children's literature about quilts and quilting can serve as a wonderful springboard to reading and writing connections, including children's own stories inspired by family quilts, scraps of cloth with special memories, and so on. You'll find literature links throughout this book, along with an annotated list of titles in the Resources section (pages 59–62). For a dictionary of quilt words plus activities to help children become comfortable with the language of quilting, see page 12. Also be sure to see pages 25–26 for a lovely folk tale from Finland, which makes an interesting math connection as well.

Social Studies

In examining antique and heirloom quilts, children will find that every stitch tells a story, enabling them to learn about American history and culture as they examine the interesting, descriptive names given to quilt patterns that have evolved over the years. They may even uncover details about their own family histories, through quilts made by relatives. See Exploring Our Heritage, pages 37–43, for related projects and activities. Be on the lookout, too, for Cultural Connections throughout the book, which introduce children to quilt customs around the world.

Experimenting with natural dyes

Science

As children investigate patterns in quilting, they'll reinforce skills that cross over from math into science, such as comparing, classifying, and measuring. Quilting is also an opportunity to explore textile science and natural dyeing. You might want to set up related science investigations as part of your quilting unit. For example, children can make their own dyes using onion skins, berries, and other natural materials, then dye swatches of fabrics. They can compare colors, explore how heat affects the dye, try setting colors (with and without alum), use a microscope to look at the weave of different fabric samples, look at changes in cloth that occur over time, experiment with the effects of the sun's light on color, and so on.

Getting Started

Try to bring some real quilts into your classroom by appealing to families as well as community resources such as craft shops, local quilting guilds, and museums. However, since not everyone has quilts in the attic or a folk art museum nearby, I've provided the next best thing: a teaching poster that pictures a glorious quilt called "Jugglery" by Paula Nadelstern and can be the start of a class quilting gallery.

Learning about the history of quilts

You do not need to be an accomplished sewer to integrate quilts into your curriculum. In fact, you don't need to sew a stitch! Most of the activities described in this book require absolutely no sewing. You can select the projects that complement your curriculum as well as your comfort level.

However, you may find, as I did, that as children complete some of the nonsewing quilting activities and explore patterns in real quilts, they become keenly interested in trying their hand at needle-and-thread quilting. A Culminating Quilt (pages 52–58) provides simple directions for creating a quilt with children—from enlisting volunteers and gathering no- and low-cost materials to planning a quilt-tying party. Suggestions for creating rewarding paper or no-sew fabric versions of the quilt are included as well.

 # Teacher Share

In addition to the many quilt projects and activities included in this book, you'll find directions for quilt projects inspired by classroom teachers and their students, including:

◆ a family heritage quilt that celebrates important events in children's lives (page 40)

◆ an author quilt that offers a special way for children to remember some of their favorite books (page 52)

◆ a poetry quilt that features children's favorite poems and their artistic interpretations of them (page 50)

Again, children can work in either paper or fabric to create similar quilts.

Detail from an author quilt

Using the Resources

The Resources section (pages 59–62) includes an annotated list of children's books mentioned throughout the book. It also lists an assortment of beautifully illustrated books about quilting, as well as video and software suggestions. Many of the books, such as those published by Dover Press, include designs and illustrations that you can photocopy and use with children for patterning activities. You may want to set up a display area so that children can easily use the books as references.

Creating quilt blocks

Launching Your Quilt Unit

A quilt is like a fabric sandwich, with a top (often patchwork), a back (usually plain fabric), and a filler (called batting). In your classroom, rather than introduce all the defining criteria, encourage children to identify the shared characteristics they find in the quilts they've seen (including any quilt pictures you have displayed) and come up with their own definitions of what makes a quilt a quilt.

Students love sewing

Quilts appeal to children for many reasons. While the overall concept of time and history is hazy for many young children, the history of quilting is often fascinating. Many historians and quilt enthusiasts have noted that quilts combine the best qualities of historical documents and personal diaries. Children enjoy unraveling the stories about real people that quilts piece together. A patch of a child's christening gown, a swatch of a worn workshirt, a piece of a daughter's outgrown sundress, snippets of old curtains—mementos in fabric are fitted together to represent what is important to the quilt's creator.

Also appealing to children is how quilts can bring people together. Until relatively recently, patchwork pieces were sewn together by hand, a slow and painstaking process. Quilting bees helped to make the time pass more quickly and increased productivity. Quilters would come together in anticipation of a wedding, birth, anniversary, housewarming, departure, or other special event in the community. They would pool their patches, threads, and skills to finish one or more quilts in a short period of time. Long-lasting friendships developed in the process.

STARTER ACTIVITIES

Use the following activities to tap children's prior knowledge about quilts, gather important information for planning inquiry-based explorations, and introduce related vocabulary.

Quilt KWL

This activity encourages children to share what they already know about quilts and would still like to learn, enabling you to assess their knowledge as you plan the quilt unit. The ideal time to do this activity is after discussing quilts and quilt history and looking together at some samples. This is a good time to take a look at the poster with children.

Materials   chart paper ◆ My Quilt KWL Chart (page 17)

To Do

1. To create a KWL chart, draw three columns on a piece of chart paper. Label them *What We Know, What We Want to Know,* and *What We Learned.*

2. Ask children to share what they already know about quilts. Record their comments in the first column. Invite them to think about what they would like to learn and fill in column two.

What We Know	What We Want to Know	What We Learned

3. As children make discoveries about quilting, they can complete the *What We Learned* column. Notice the depth and detail of their comments here, useful for assessment purposes.

4. Ask children what they would still like to know about quilting. As an extension, partners or small groups can investigate areas of common interest.

5. Follow up by having children fill in reproducible page 17 as the unit progresses. At the end of the unit, these will provide an excellent means of self-assessment.

A Quilting Dictionary

Use the reproducible to introduce new words. Although there is quite a bit of specialized quilting vocabulary, children will internalize it quickly.

Materials Vocabulary Patchwork (page 18)

To Do

1. Enlarge reproducible page 18 and display it where everyone can see it. As you introduce quilting words in activities and discussions, print them in the squares.

Encourage children to suggest words to add to the patchwork. Remind them that they can use the chart as reference for their writing.

2. Distribute the reproducible and invite older children to keep their own Vocabulary Patchworks, adding words as they notice them in reference materials or discussions.

QUILTING VOCABULARY

Here are some of the ABCs of quilting to get your Vocabulary Patchwork started. Words in **bold** are quilt pattern names or types.

A **album quilt; Amish quilt; Anvil**

B backing; batting; bee; block; border

C calico; **charm quilt; Churn Dash; Crazy quilt;** cut

D design; diagonal; **Double Wedding Ring**

E **Eight Hands Round**

F Fabric; **Flying Geese; freedom quilt; friendship quilt**

G geometric shapes; grid

H **Hawaiian quilt; Hearts and Hands;** heirloom; heritage

I indigo

J **Jacob's Ladder**

K **Kite's Tail**

L lattice; layout; **Log Cabin**

M **map quilt; Maple Leaf**

N needle; notions

O **Ohio Star**

P patchwork; pattern

Q quilt

R rows; running stitch

S **sampler quilt;** sentimental value; sew; stitch; **story quilt;** symmetry

T thread; tied quilt; **Tree of Life; Tumbling Blocks**

U **Underground Railroad**

V **Variable Star**

W **wedding quilt; Windmill**

X *X* for cross-stitch

Y **Yankee Puzzle**

Z **Zigzag**

Quilts in the Attic

Reinforce quilting vocabulary with this adaptation of the traditional memory game, "In My Grandmother's Attic." Any size group can play.

To Do

1. After children become familiar with some quilt terminology, sit in a circle and have the first player begin by naming a quilt word that begins with **A**, such as **album quilt.**

2. The next player adds a **B** word to the list and recites both words; for example, **album quilt, block.** The game continues as each player adds a quilt word beginning with the next letter of the alphabet. No one is eliminated from the game for missing a word—just skip to the next player if someone is stumped. Will anyone in the class be able to recite 26 quilt words, ending with **Zigzag?** They'll have fun trying!

GETTING TO KNOW QUILTS

Next to the visual beauty of quilt designs, perhaps the most fascinating aspect of them is the variety of quilt names that the patterns have inspired. As children study the quilt pictured on the poster, invite them to guess how the quilt got their names. Share the explanations here and follow up with any related investigations that give children a chance to explore American history, culture, and more.

Anvil: Tool used by a blacksmith. This is just one of the early American tools children can research.

Barn raising: Community members would work together to build one another's new barns and turn the day into a social event as well.

Churn Dash

Churn Dash: This refers to butter churning, which children may like to try themselves. It can lead to interesting research on how other kinds of foods were prepared in the olden days.

Flying Geese: Geese were an important farm animal, valued for their meat, eggs, and feathers. The quilt pattern's triangles are reminiscent of the V-shape of a migratory flock.

Flying Geese

Log Cabin: The log cabin was a basic type of dwelling for many pioneer families. Children might design quilt blocks that represent their homes and investigate other types of homes around the world (materials, shapes, and so on).

Maple Leaf: This pattern symbolizes the maple tree, the sap of which was collected, cooked, and made into syrup and candy. Children can research trees in their area. How do they help? *(by supplying shade, wood for homes, oxygen for the air, and so on)* How might children symbolize a tree in quilt pattern?

Log Cabin

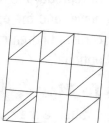
Maple Leaf

Nebraska Windmill: Windmills were, and still are, an important source of energy on farms and can lead to science investigations on energy.

Ohio Star: Variations on this star appear in dozens of other quilt patterns. What did the star represent to people long ago?

Old Tippecanoe: This pattern immortalized the nickname of America's ninth president, William Henry Harrison. Who were other presidents during the 1800s?

Ohio Star

Storm at Sea: Since many new Americans arrived here after a lengthy ocean voyage, the image of a storm at sea is one most would never forget. What were some of the other struggles of immigrants?

Tree of Life: This universal symbol represents the sense of hope many pioneering Americans tried to maintain during difficult times. How do the difficulties faced by people today compare? Children can design their own quilt patterns to symbolize hope in their world.

Underground Railroad: Learning more about this pattern will help students understand how some southern slaves escaped to freedom.

Two children's books that invite students to discover more about quilt names are *Eight Hands Round* by Ann Whitford Paul and *Q Is for Quilt* by Gwen Marston. Both of these ABC books take readers through the alphabet, introducing 26 quilt patterns with information on the names and illustrations. After sharing these books with children, play Quilt Match.

 # Quilt Match

This game helps children become more familiar with quilt pattern blocks and begin to associate them with their names.

Materials
Quilt Blocks (pages 19–21) ◆ crayons ◆ scissors

To Do
Prepare playing cards and boards. Every group of three players will need two sets of reproducible pages 19–21: one set to use as a bingo-like game board for each player and the other set to be cut apart, shuffled together, and used as playing cards. Children can color their playing cards and game boards. Lamination is optional.

To Play
1. Shuffle the cards and place them facedown in the middle of a table. Each child in the group receives a different game board.

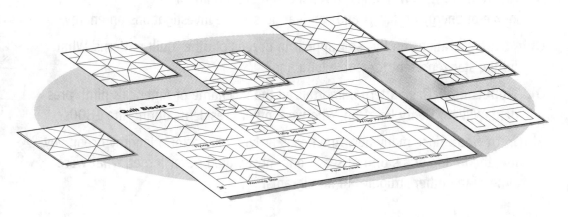

2. Children take turns drawing a card and trying to match the card to a pattern block on their game board, using picture and word clues. If the card does not match the board, it is returned to the bottom of the deck.

3. Play continues until one player matches all the pattern blocks on his or her game board.

Variations

◆ Build literacy skills by inviting children to put the cards in ABC order.

◆ Reinforce patterning skills by having children use manipulatives to replicate the designs.

◆ Challenge children to make new games, showing new quilts on cards they make themselves.

Pocket Chart Classification

As children gain familiarity with the names and appearances of various quilt patterns, they will begin to see relationships among some of the different names and can look for ways to classify them. For example, one group of first graders made connections between categories from their life science studies and classification of quilt names: *things that are/were alive; things that never were alive; things that came from something alive*. When children reinforce learning in one curriculum area by applying skills and knowledge to a second area, the results are impressive!

This game invites children to put their classification skills to work as they look for relationships and make connections. You might set up this activity at a learning center, for children to complete independently or in small groups, then follow up with a class discussion. Sometimes a quilt name or pattern will fit in more than one category, which can make for lively discussion.

Materials   pocket chart ◆ sentence strips ◆ Quilt Blocks (pages 19–21)

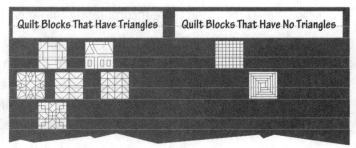

To Do

1. Section off a large pocket chart with headings for categories of your choice; for example, **Quilt Blocks That Have Triangles, Quilt Blocks That Have No Triangles.**

2. Photocopy one set of reproducible pages 19–21. Laminate if desired and cut apart. What other classification categories can children develop?

3. Invite children to organize the cards in the pocket chart, based on the character-istics they represent.

4. Extend learning by encouraging children to research additional quilt pattern names. (See Literature Link, page 14.) Let them make new quilt name cards to classify.

 # Building on Shapes

Children build on geometry concepts as they explore shapes and pat-terns in quilt making.

Materials
½- or 1-inch Grid Paper (pages 22–23) ◆ colored pencils ◆ construction paper

To Do

1. Discuss how quilt designers combined familiar elements from their lives with ideas from their own imaginations to create beautiful new patterns. Talk about how quilt makers joined together simple geometric shapes such as squares and triangles to create representations of objects rather than exact images.

2. Brainstorm a list of familiar items from children's everyday lives that might make interesting quilt patterns. Post the list where children can easily refer to it.

3. Model the process of creating a representation of an item on the list by coloring in geometric shapes on grid paper. Then give children reproducible page 22 or 23, and let them try.

4. While children are working, circulate through the room and encourage them to talk about their design process. Invite them to show you what elements of quilt design, such as symmetry and balance, they are incorporating into their patterns.

5. After children complete their designs, invite them to create names for their patterns and write his-tories of their patterns. You can share *Eight Hands Round* by Ann Whitford Paul as inspira-tion for names and histories.

6. Mount children's designs and histories on con-struction paper and display in the quilt gallery or bind into a big book for your classroom collection.

TIP

Have extra sheets of grid paper on hand. The cre-ative process often has several false starts!

My Quilt KWL Chart

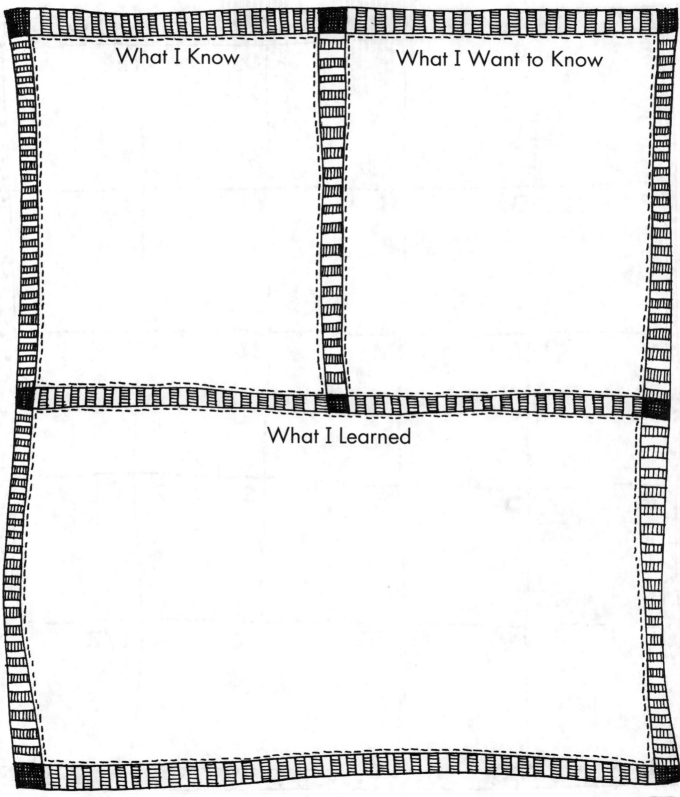

What I Know

What I Want to Know

What I Learned

Name_____

Vocabulary Patchwork

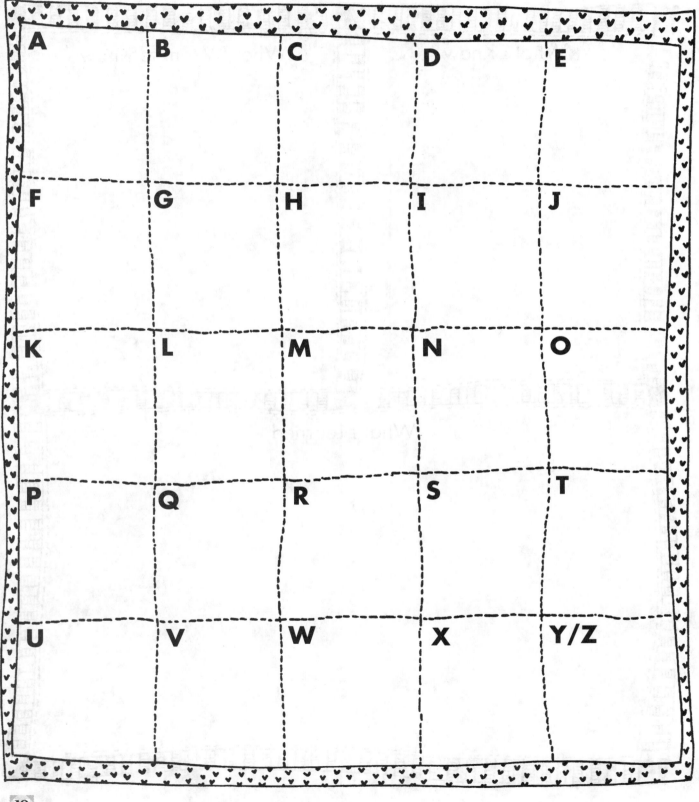

Quilt Blocks 1

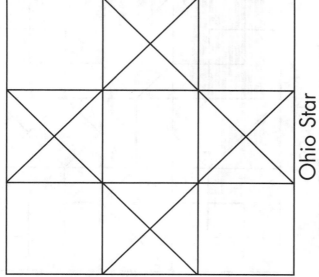

Ohio Star

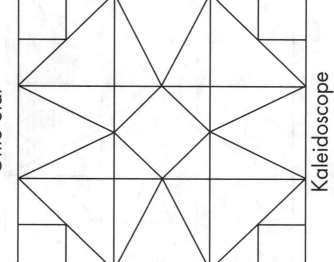

Kaleidoscope

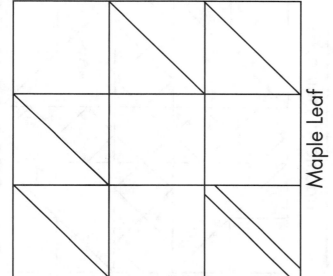

Maple Leaf

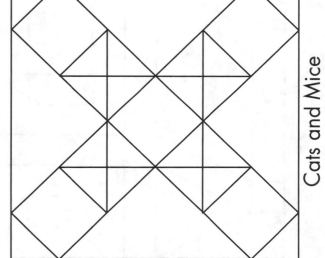

Cats and Mice

Postage Stamp

Zigzag

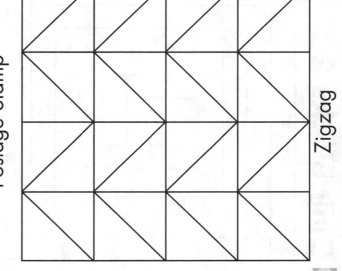

19

Quilt Blocks 2

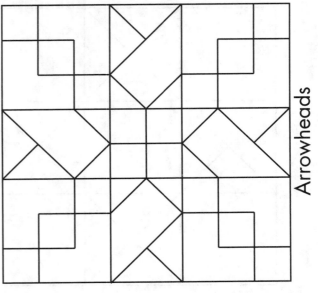

Sunset

Arrowheads

Traditional House

Bird's Nest

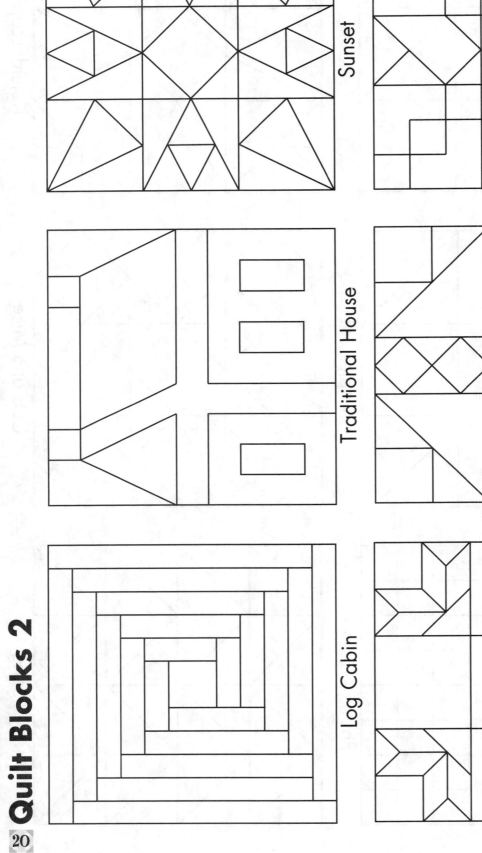

Log Cabin

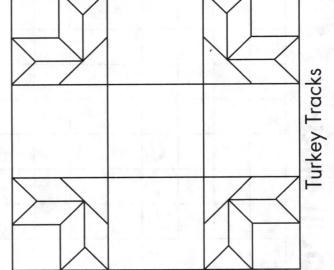

Turkey Tracks

Quilt Blocks 3

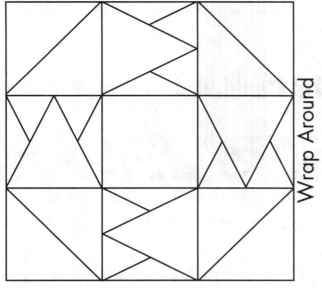

Wrap Around

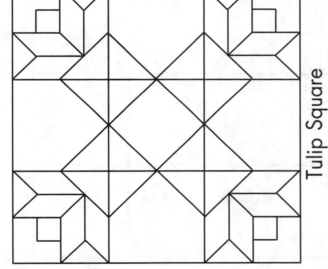

Tulip Square

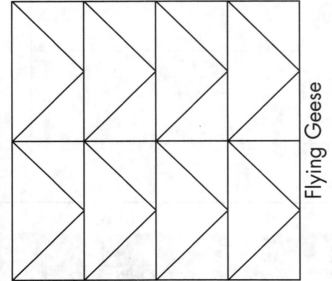

Flying Geese

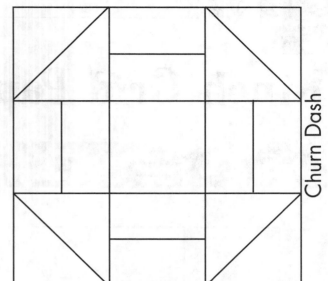

Churn Dash

Four Arrows

Morning Star

1-inch Grid Paper

My pattern is called _____.

½-inch Grid Paper

My pattern is called _____.

Patchwork Math

Every quilter is a mathematician. Understanding how shapes fit together to form other shapes requires fundamentals of geometry. Visualizing how those shapes can form a balanced pattern means understanding symmetry in design, an important mathematical concept. Calculating and measuring necessary yardage, estimating how many patches of each shape and color to cut, counting how many stitches to the inch, figuring the cost of materials and notions needed to finish the project—yes, a quilter definitely works with numbers! In this chapter, you will find many hands-on interactive lessons and activities rich with mathematical skills, vocabulary, and applications.

Quilters are mathematicians

A Folk Tale From Finland

The charming folk tale on pages 25–26 is a great way to help children recognize the strong connection between quilting and math. In the Scandinavian countries, where winters are long and hard and the nights are cold, quilts have long been an important household item. Locate Finland on a map with children, then share "Aili's Quilt." Follow up with an activity that will put children's problem-solving skills to work.

FOLLOW UP Invite children to share their solutions to Aili's quilt problem. How would they make sure the quilt would cover Kalle from head to toe? Children might like to act out the story, including an ending that demonstrates their suggestions. For children who cannot read the story independently, you can record the story on an audiocassette and let children use stick or hand puppets or felt board cutouts to make the story come alive. Older children can write their own scripted versions of the story to use in readers' theater or skits. A simple staging of "Aili's Quilt" would make perfect entertainment at the end of a quilt-tying party, too (page 55).

Aili's Quilt

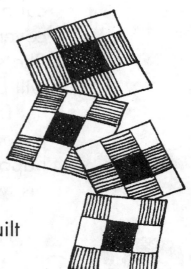

Long ago, in a little Finnish town named Holmola, lived a husband and wife who were completely devoted to each other. Aili, the wife, had just completed a patchwork quilt as a birthday gift for her husband, Kalle. Aili had worked for weeks, cutting and piecing together colorful wool scraps to make the most beautiful quilt that anyone in Holmola had ever seen.

Kalle was delighted with his gift. "What a crafty gal I married!" he exclaimed. That night, as always, the wind began to whistle through the cracks in the walls of their little house. To warm himself, Kalle jumped into bed and pulled the new quilt up over his neck and ears. But guess what happened?

"Oh, no! My feet stick out!" he cried. "My quilt is too short!" He turned this way and that, trying to cover his whole body, but there were his feet, as cold as ever! Shivering, he finally fell asleep.

The next morning he told Aili about the problem with the quilt. "Hmmm," she said. "So it covered your ears and neck but your feet stuck out? Show me which end covered your neck and ears."

After Kalle showed her how the quilt covered him, Aili thought and thought. "I know just what to do!" she said to herself. Then Aili took out her best scissors and

cut a full row of patchwork blocks from the end that covered Kalle's neck. And what do you think she did? She sewed it to the other end of the quilt! Now his feet will be warm! she thought.

That night, Kalle again climbed into bed and pulled the quilt over his neck and ears. But guess what happened? Yes, you are right, my friend! There were his two feet and ten toes shivering in the cold. Again!

The next morning he told Aili about the problem. Aili thought even longer and harder about the problem. Can you guess what she did?

Yes, you are right again, my friend! Aili took her sharp scissors and cut off another row of patchwork blocks from the end of the quilt that covered her poor cold husband's neck and ears, and she stitched it tightly to the other end of the quilt. Pleased with herself, she thought of how toasty warm Kalle would be that night.

But once again, when Kalle pulled up the quilt that night, his feet nearly turned blue with cold, while his neck and ears were snug and warm.

Every night for a week, Aili lopped off a row of patchwork blocks from one end of the quilt and sewed it to the foot end. And every morning for a week, Kalle shook his head sadly and pointed to his poor cold feet. Finally, Aili gave up on that quilt and decided to make a new quilt, one big enough to cover Kalle from head to toe.

Do you have any suggestions for Aili?

Quilt Close-up

It's time to take a closer look at quilts. Now children will be looking at them as mathematicians, working cooperatively as they search for common aspects—shapes, colors, and patterns—in the quilts they see.

Materials

Patchwork Patterns poster ◆ Quilt Close-up (page 33)

To Do

1. Invite small groups of children to explore the poster, then use it to fill in reproducible page 33.

2. After all the groups have had the opportunity to complete their reproducible pages, bring the class together to share their findings. What shapes, patterns, and colors did children discover in the quilt? Which quilt blocks were their favorites?

3. As an extension, take snapshots of actual quilts, focusing on individual blocks. Give each group one of the photos and another copy of reproducible page 33, and let them repeat the activity with these quilt-block photos.

> **TIP**
> Laminate the poster to make it more durable.

QUILTING MANIPULATIVES

These manipulatives are ideal for developing patterning skills and making facsimiles of quilt patches. (You will probably need three or four buckets to supply a class of 20 children.)

◆ Color tiles are approximately 1 inch square and ¼ inch thick. They come in red, yellow, green, and blue.

◆ Rainbow cubes are 1-centimeter cubes that come in six different colors: orange, yellow, blue, green, pink, and purple.

◆ In place of commercial manipulatives, you can make your own. Simply color, laminate, and cut apart the 1-inch Grid Paper (page 22). Or have adults help create shapes to use with the Quilt-Block Workmat (page 36). Store in resealable plastic bags.

Color Tile Patterns

As children's interest in quilt patterns blossoms, use color tiles to explore symmetry and color design.

Materials

color tiles ◇ 1-inch Grid Paper, optional (page 22)

To Do

A	B	A	B	A	B
B	A	B	A	B	A
A	B	A	B	A	B
B	A	B	A	B	A
A	B	A	B	A	B
B	A	B	A	B	A

1. Gather children in a circle on the floor and model a basic AB pattern with the color tiles. After completing one row of five or six tiles, continue the pattern on the next two rows and ask children what they notice. After discussing responses, finish the pattern to form a complete square, with five or six rows, depending on how many tiles you started with in the first row.

2. Invite children to notice the resulting diagonal and vertical patterns. Start another AB pattern, this time letting children take turns completing the square.

3. Let children follow up in small groups or pairs, creating their own pattern squares. When children feel comfortable with two colors, encourage them to extend their patterning with three colors and then four colors.

A	B	C	A	B	C
B	C	A	B	C	A
C	A	B	C	A	B
A	B	C	A	B	C
B	C	A	B	C	A
C	A	B	C	A	B

A	B	C	D	A	B	C	D
B	C	D	A	B	C	D	A
C	D	A	B	C	D	A	B
D	A	B	C	D	A	B	C
A	B	C	D	A	B	C	D
B	C	D	A	B	C	D	A
C	D	A	B	C	D	A	B
D	A	B	C	D	A	B	C

4. Challenge children to create patterns with colors that radiate out from the center. Model this; it *is* challenging. You can help children get started with this pattern by suggesting that they use only three colors. Place the first color and then show them how each side of that color must be touched by the second color.

5. Encourage children to explore other combinations. They'll have fun challenging one another to replicate the patterns they create by listening to verbal clues. Be sure to have resource books with quilt photographs on hand for reference.

TIP

Children can record favorite pattern combinations on grid paper (pages 22–23), using colored pencils to fill in the shapes. They can also paste paper construction squares in place to replicate the patterns.

 In *A Cloak for the Dreamer* by Aileen Friedman, the properties of geometric shapes become vitally important as three sons attempt to make patchwork cloaks for the archduke to wear on an important journey. Through trial and error, Misha, the youngest son, learns lessons about patchwork geometry—and lessons about himself, too.

Children will enjoy discussing issues raised in the story: What do the patchwork cloaks designed by each of the brothers reveal about their personalities?

 # Rainbow Cube Combinations

For more color and pattern possibilities, let children experiment with 1-centimeter rainbow cubes as they did color tiles. The smaller size and additional colors of rainbow cubes give children a different medium to produce quilt block patterns.

Materials
rainbow cubes ◈ 9-Patch Workmat (page 34) ◈ colored markers in cubes' colors

To Do

1. Allow time for children to freely explore with the cubes and enjoy their colors, then have them sort the cubes by color.

2. Let children select cubes in three different colors. Ask them how many different combinations they think they can make with these colors. Then let them try to make as many different nine-patch squares with their rainbow cubes as possible—a terrific challenge! Children can try out their patterns on the workmat with the cubes, then record their findings with colored markers.

Patterning with rainbow cubes

P = Purple   G = Green   Y = Yellow

P	G	P
G	P	G
P	G	P

P	P	P
P	Y	P
P	P	P

G	Y	G
Y	P	Y
G	Y	G

P	G	Y
G	Y	P
Y	P	G

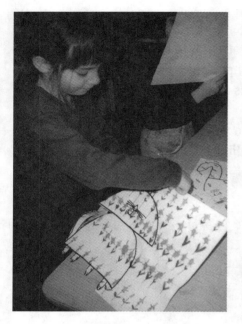

 Everyone loves *The Gingham Dog and the Calico* Cat by Eugene Field. It is a funny poem about two stuffed animals in an antique shop who get in a fight in the middle of the night. Children will certainly recognize gingham as a common pattern built out of squares like the tiles and cubes they have been using. As for calico, it was and is the fundamental type of fabric used in many quilts. This charming picture book and accompanying activity provide an enjoyable way to build on what children have learned.

After sharing the book and looking at calico and gingham scraps for reference, give childen drawing paper and markers and let them design their own calico or gingham, completely covering the paper. They can sketch pictures of dogs, cats, or other favorite animals on their designs, then carefully cut out the calico and gingham animals to use as puppets in a dramatic retelling of the story.

Geoboard Quilting

Children can use geoboards to replicate existing quilting designs and create original ones.

Materials

geoboards ◇ rubber bands in assorted colors ◇ Geoboard Workmat (page 35) ◇ colored pencils or markers

To Do

TIP

Share short segments of *Eight Hands Round* by Ann Whitford Paul to give children a sense of how quilt pattern names grow out of objects and events from people's lives.

1. If possible, provide samples of black and white instructional quilting diagrams—the kind quilters would use as a guide to fit pieces together. Good sources are quilting pattern magazines or how-to quilt books, such as Georgia Bonesteel's *Lap Quilting* and Elizabeth F. Nyhan's *Treasury of Patchwork Quilt Sets*.

Quilting with geoboards

2. Let children select patterns that appeal to them, then use colored rubber bands either to re-create the designs or construct original patterns based on these designs. Most children will extend from the replicated pattern into original territory. They will have a wonderful time naming these original patterns, too.

3. Invite childen to name their quilt patterns. Display their geoboard patterns for a few days. Then, since you may need the geoboards for other math activities, take snapshots, label them, and make them part of a growing display. Or let children record their designs on reproducible page 35 using colored pencils or markers.

Re-creating a pattern on a geoboard

Quilt-Block Manipulatives

You can add to the manipulatives you offer children with these appealing quilt-pattern pieces (a good send-home job for adult volunteers).

Materials

assorted fabric scraps ◆ fusible webbing ◆ tagboard
◆ Quilt-Block Workmat (page 36) ◆ glue

To Do

1. Iron assorted calico fabrics onto tagboard using fusible webbing (available at fabric stores).

2. Using the Quilt-Block Workmat as a guide, cut the tagboard-backed fabric into square and triangle shapes.

3. Invite children to mix and match the fabric shapes into dozens of combinations on the workmat. When they hit upon a design they love, they can glue the shapes to the mat for you to display.

Designing quilt blocks with a related activity from Box It and Bag It Math/Kindergarten *(Salem, OR: Math Learning Center, 1988)*

Quilting Story Problems

If you get into the habit of "talking math" with children when looking at quilt designs, story problems will be a natural outgrowth. Writing— and solving—original quilting story problems can be fun for the whole class. Be sure to have a selection of manipulatives on hand to help children visualize the quilts in the problems. Here are a few problems at various skill levels, just to get you started.

SAMPLE STORY PROBLEM 1

Zachary's parents decided to make him a baby quilt before he was born, and he still likes to use it! The border of Zachary's baby quilt is 9 blocks wide and 12 blocks long. How many blocks do you think are in the border? How many blocks do you think are in the whole quilt?

SAMPLE STORY PROBLEM 2

Mrs. Buchberg's class made a beautiful quilt using blocks of fabric they printed with *adinkra* symbols, surrounded by a colorful border. There are 24 blocks in the quilt. 16 blocks touch the border. How many blocks do not touch the border? (For more on *adinkra* cloths, see Cultural Connection, page 49.)

SAMPLE STORY PROBLEM 3

Two classes would both like to make friendship quilts using eight-inch-square blocks. Each class has 24 students and one teacher. They would like to cut their blocks from an old sheet that is 66 by 96 inches. Using words, pictures, and numbers, figure out if the sheet is big enough for both classes and their teachers to cut blocks for everyone.

Quilt Close-up

**Look at the quilt carefully. Choose your favorite block.
Use it to answer these questions.**

1. What is the name of your quilt block? _____

_____

2. Why do you think it has this name? _____

_____

3. What colors do you see in it? _____

_____

4. What shapes do you see in it? _____

_____

5. Draw your quilt block in
the box. Then color it in.

Name_____

9-Patch Workmat

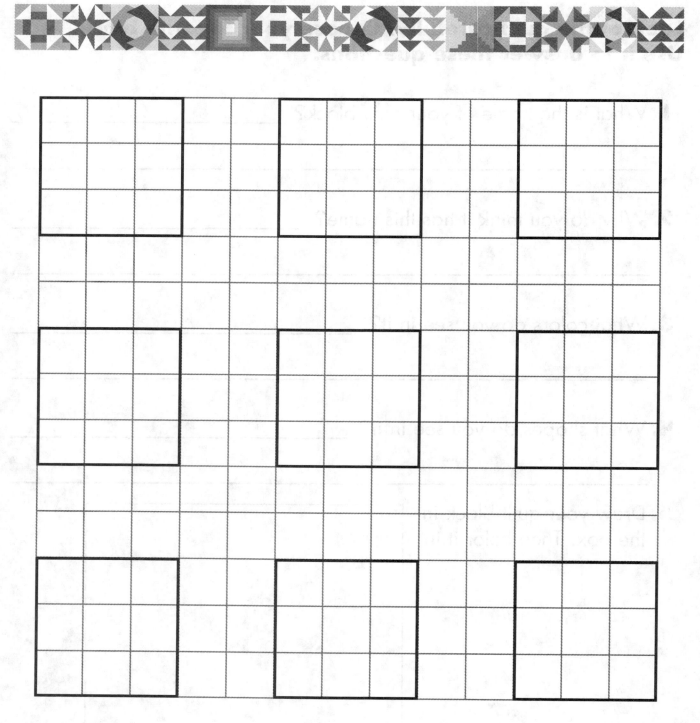

Geoboard Workmat

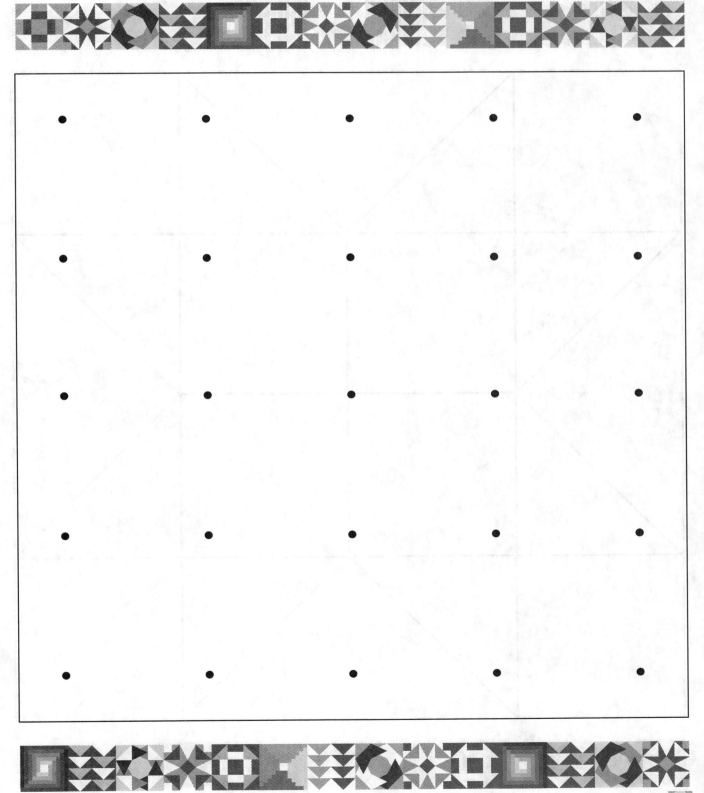

Quilt-Block Workmat

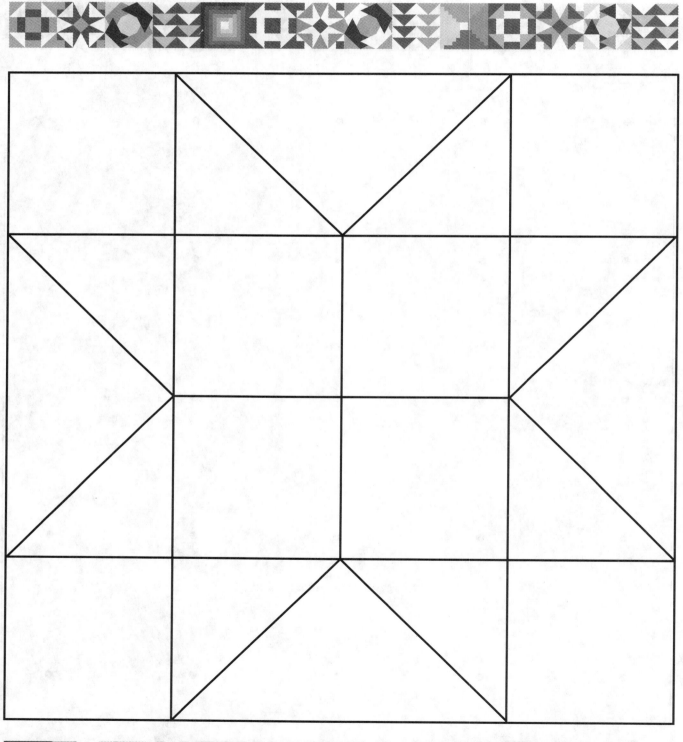

Exploring Our Heritage

Quilts bring a concrete and fascinating focus to the themes of family and community in the social studies curriculum. The activities that follow encourage children to use creative and higher-order thinking skills to explore family and social history. In preparation for these activities, make your classroom environment as rich as possible with actual quilts—especially those that have an interesting history and family legacy children can unearth.

A good place to begin your search for quilts is with children's families. Send home a note explaining the quilt theme unit and inviting parents to share family quilts with the class for a day or two. Parents or grandparents might like to visit, too, to share details about the quilts' histories. Next, reach out into your community to help bring quilts to children—or children to the quilts! You may be surprised at the interest your young quilting enthusiasts spark in nearby senior centers, fabric and quilting shops, and museums.

Add the quilts to your classroom display (the poster, children's own quilt patterns, and so on), along with quilt resource books. And don't forget about the Internet. If you have access to the World Wide Web, you can bring a virtual quilt shop or museum exhibit right into your classroom.

KINDS OF QUILTS

As you explore the history of quilts with children, be on the lookout for quilts that fit these categories. You might copy this information on chart paper, so that children can more easily identify kinds of quilts they see.

A Friendship quilt

Friendship quilts usually feature a large number of blocks, each one made by a different quilter in the bee and later joined together. These quilts were offered as gifts to welcome people to the community, to say good-bye if they were moving, or to celebrate milestone wedding anniversaries.

Wedding quilts generally contained all-over patterns such as Log Cabin (to represent the new household), Double Wedding Ring, or Hearts and Hands.

Album quilts and **sampler quilts** feature many different blocks, each with a different pattern. Patterns formed with geometric shapes were usually appliquéed.

Charm quilts are true scrap quilts—no two patches are alike. In order to achieve such fabric variety, friends and neighbors often exchanged charm squares.

Amish quilts feature solid fabrics rather than calicos and prints, reflecting the simple lifestyle of the Amish sect.

Crazy quilts, made of haphazardly overlapping scraps of odd-shaped silks, satins, and velvets, became the rage during the Victorian era. With the invention of household appliances, women spent less time on domestic chores and more on political and social causes. It was not uncommon, beginning in the late 1800s, to see quilts with slogans and images built into the design, supporting presidential candidates, prohibition, and woman suffrage.

Freedom quilts helped runaway slaves move safely north. Log Cabin quilts made with a dark square in the center were commonly hung along with other household quilts outside safe houses on the Underground Railroad. Escaped slaves needed only to glance at the clothesline to know where to find food, shelter, and aid. A book to share on this moving topic is *Sweet Clara and the Freedom Quilt* by Deborah Hopkinson.

TIP

Make sure children wash and dry their hands before touching a quilt. Explain that old fabrics can be fragile, and that dirt and perspiration from our hands can damage them.

The National AIDS Quilt, with thousands of panels, commemorates loved ones who have died from AIDS. Each panel tells an important story about the life of an individual person, and as a whole, the quilt sends a powerful message of grief, hope, and urgency.

Piece It Together

Quilts are a wonderful record of history. As a warm-up to this cooperative learning activity, ask children to name other objects, such as postcards, diaries, and records, that help tell us about the past. What are some ways that children in years to come will learn about today's children's own lives?

Introduce the activity by explaining that children will become detectives, using clues from a real quilt to piece together details about the quilter's life. When actual details about a particular quilt's history are unknown, children can make educated guesses about its background.

Materials
quilt ◆ flat sheet (or large, clean cloth) ◆ Piece It Together (pages 42–43)

To Do

1. Spread the quilt on the floor, on top of a clean flat sheet. Have children sit on the floor around the quilt. Together, look at various visual clues the quilt provides about the quilt, quilter, and era. Use these questions to guide your discussion:

   ◆ What is the overall condition of this quilt? (Examine frays, rips, stains, mended areas, fading, and so on.)

   ◆ What can you tell about the age of the quilt? (Examine the stitching on the quilt. Is it machine stitching or hand stitching?)

   ◆ Do you think this was a scrap quilt? (Examine the colors and designs of individual pieces, as well as the weight and quality of the fabrics themselves.)

   ◆ What do the colors and prints tell you about the quilter?

   ◆ Can you tell if this quilt was made for a special occasion or a particular person? (Look at the pattern blocks in the quilt.)

Quilt block

2. Let children work in pairs or small groups to record other observations on reproducible pages 42–43.

3. To extend learning, invite children to select another quilt (or picture of a quilt) and, using known facts, deductions, or imagined details, tell the story of the quilt. If the quilt could talk, what stories would it tell about its life?

 Family Heritage Quilt

After reading *The Keeping Quilt* by Patricia Polacco and other stories about quilts, Melissa Kile, a kindergarten teacher at Riner Elementary School in Riner, Virginia, and her students were inspired to create their own quilt, in cooperation with families. With a little planning and some help from parent volunteers, they pieced together a quilt that captures important events in their lives. Here's how you can create your own Family Heritage quilt (with or without sewing).

Materials

meaningful fabric scraps ◆ index cards ◆ glue ◆ quilting materials ◆ *The Keeping Quilt* ◆ three-ring binder ◆ large bag

To Do

1. Ask each child to bring in a piece of clothing (or scrap) with some sort of memory, such as an outgrown favorite dress or a worn baby blanket. Cut a 12-inch square from the cloth. Cut a smaller sample from each piece of cloth for each child. Ask children to glue their smaller cloth samples to index cards and write their names on the backs. Children can use these to help locate their squares on the finished quilt.

2. Ask adult volunteers to piece together the squares (in class, if possible, so that children can view the progress), adding batting and backing if desired. (Other options are to use fusible webbing, available at fabric stores, to attach quilt squares to a backing, or simply to arrange fabric squares on paper and glue in place.)

3. Put the finished quilt in a sturdy bag, along with a copy of *The Keeping Quilt* and a three-ring binder with plenty of paper. Send the quilt kit home to a different family each night. Ask that each family look at the quilt together, identify the child's square, and write a story in the notebook about the cloth's history.

In *Patchwork Tales* by Susan L. Roth and Ruth Phang, a grandmother shares with her granddaughter the family history behind the blocks in a patchwork quilt. Invite children to tell stories from their lives in quilt squares, using paper or fabric scraps pasted to construction paper squares. Have them write or dictate stories to go with their squares. Compile into a class Patchwork Tales book.

 # Patchwork Community

In *Patchwork Island* by Karla Kuskin, a mother expresses her love for her baby and the environment where they live by stitching the landscape of their beautiful island into a magnificent patchwork quilt. Use this book as a springboard to designing quilts that represent something special about where children live. Children will not be able to make a scaled and perfectly accurate patchwork representation of the community, of course, but the process of visualizing the geography of their neighborhood, talking about it, and representing it in the placement of their cut-out likenesses makes a fascinating social studies project.

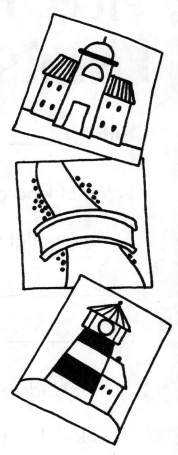

Materials

chart paper ◆ construction paper (or felt and fabric) ◆ scissors ◆ butcher paper (or a bedsheet or other large piece of fabric) ◆ glue

To Do

1. Have children begin by creating a list of landmarks in their neighborhood or community, such as their homes, school, public library, favorite shop, and parks and playgrounds, as well as important geographical features such as streams, lakes, and hills.

2. Ask children to cut out the shapes of their landmarks from paper, felt, or fabric.

3. Let children arrange their shapes on butcher paper. Paste in place.

 Faith Ringgold tells stories on quilts using a combination of pictures and words. Introduce this technique by sharing some of her books, such as *Tar Beach* and *Aunt Harriet and the Underground Railroad in the Sky*, as well as the biography *Faith Ringgold* by Robyn Montana Turner. For a historical look at the African-American tradition of story quilting, read *Stitching Stars: The Story Quilts of Harriet Powers* by Mary Lyons. Then invite children to create their own story quilts.

◆ Ask children to think of stories from their lives they'd like to tell in a quilt. Family members can help by talking about memorable incidents with their children.

◆ Discuss ways of representing children's stories in a series of pictures. Provide 8-inch squares of paper for children to tell their stories. (Each child might use 9 squares to make a three-by-three quilt.)

◆ Have children arrange their quilt blocks on butcher paper and glue in place. Display children's story quilts along with some of Faith Ringgold's books.

Piece It Together

Quilt _____

1. What kind of condition is the quilt in? What does it tell you about

how it might have been used? _____

_____

_____

2. What kinds of fabrics were used? Plain or fancy? Cottons or silks?

Colorful or pale? What clues do the fabrics give about the quilter?

_____

_____

_____

3. What kind of quilt design do you see? Simple or complex?

How even are the stitches? How experienced was the quilter?

_____

_____

_____

Name_____

Piece It Together (continued)

4. Look at the type of pattern. Can you identify it? Can you tell if this

was made for a special occasion or person? _____

_____

_____

_____

5. Is this a very old quilt? How can you tell? _____

_____

_____

_____

6. What other things do you notice about the quilt? What clues do

they provide about the quilt's past and the quilter? _____

_____

_____

_____

_____

Cross-Curricular Quilting Connections

Experimenting with a variety of arts and crafts media will enable every child to find a comfortable quilting niche. Some children may not yet have acquired sufficient small-motor dexterity to wield a needle and thread comfortably, but they may be very successful in translating quilt designs onto paper, or even a computer screen. The cross-curricular projects detailed in this chapter invite children to explore quilting with photos, prints, paintings, poems, and more.

As you consider the various quilt projects, keep in mind that the specific materials you and the children select are less important than the process itself. Think of your project time as an opportunity for children creatively to manipulate pattern, shape, and color. Be sure to allow plenty of time for children to discuss the layout of their quilts. As they move the pieces around on the table or floor, they'll gain experience with counting, odd and even numbers, and balance and symmetry.

NO-SEW FABRIC QUILTING

With some inexpensive fusible webbing products, available at fabric stores, children can use fabric for quilting projects—no sewing required. You can also experiment with using craft glue to attach quilt pieces to a backing and puffy craft paint to outline the patterns. The small bottles it comes in are easily managed by even your youngest quilt enthusiasts. Fabric crayon quilts, like the one shown here, are another appealing option.

 # Huppah Celebration Canopy

A huppah (or chuppah) is a traditional canopy under which Jewish wedding ceremonies are performed. In *The Keeping Quilt* by Patricia Polacco, an immigrant family's quilt, which had been passed down from generation to generation, is used as a wedding huppah, with great sentimental significance to all. Many modern-day Jewish couples are building on this tradition, using a quilt for the canopy.

You can adapt this tradition for special classroom celebrations using a fabric or paper quilt children make. Hang the quilt from the ceiling pattern-side down (or drape it across the walls in a corner) to form a special events canopy. Use this as a place of honor for guest speakers to sit when visiting your class; set up your author's chair here for writing workshop; let birthday children blow out their candles here; and be sure to take a group photo of your class under the huppah. In the tradition of the Jewish wedding huppah, it celebrates togetherness and is said to bring health and happiness to all who go under it!

 # Our Class in a Quilt

This is an excellent beginner's project, perfect for the opening weeks of school or any time of year.

Materials
drawing paper (cut into 5-inch squares or larger) ◇ pocket mirrors ◇ crayons, markers, colored pencils ◇ construction paper

To Do
1. Ask each child to draw a self-portrait on one of the squares (doing sketches on scrap paper first, if desired).

2. Assemble squares on a bulletin board in a checkerboard fashion, alternating face squares with squares of solid color construction paper. If desired, make a border with strips of a contrasting color.

Variations
◆ Instead of paper, cut squares from an old light-colored sheet. Use fabric crayons (available at craft and variety stores) on white paper to draw the faces. Iron crayon drawings onto the fabric and staple the fabric face squares directly to the bulletin board as described above, forming a checkerboard design with paper or calico fabric squares. Later, adult volunteers can sew these into a quilt.

◆ Instead of drawing themselves, let partners draw portraits of each other.

TIP
Have pocket mirrors available to encourage kids to examine their faces and build in lots of detail.

Alphabet and Number Quilt

Add to the print environment in your classroom with an alphabet quilt designed by children.

Materials

drawing paper, cut into squares ◇ crayons, markers, paints ◇ craft paper ◇ glue

To Do

1. Randomly assign each child one letter of the alphabet. Have children carefully print the upper- and lowercase forms of their letters and illustrate. For example, a child illustrating the letter *B* might draw a bee, ball, banana, and bird.

2. For a number quilt, let children choose objects and draw the corresponding number of them, or think of an object that represents the number (such as a tricycle to go with 3, a box of eggs for 12, and so on).

3. Have children decide on an arrangement for their letter and number quilts, then paste in place. They can use paper or fabric strips to create quilt borders, then display their work on a classroom wall or bulletin board.

Biography Quilt

In connection with a focus on biographies, children can create quilt squares that represent people they are researching.

An interesting mathematical—and practical—challenge for children is to decide whether to make one larger quilt or several smaller ones. Depending on the size of your class, the latter option may be easier to manage. Older students can measure and arrange spaces themselves.

Materials

10-inch paper squares ◇ paper, felt, or fabric scraps (old magazines to cut up, yarn, buttons, craft eyes, synthetic craft hair, and other findings may also be useful) ◇ craft paper ◇ glue

To Do

Using felt or fabric scraps, let each child create an image on a paper quilt square representing a person in history. (For example, a child could represent Harriet Tubman by showing stars in the shape of the "drinking gourd" or Little Dipper.)

Hand- and Footprint Quilt

This paper quilting process gives children the opportunity to produce simple yet beautiful results.

Materials

tempera or textile paint ◇ paintbrushes ◇ white paper or fabric squares ◇ crayons (or fabric crayons) ◇ butcher or craft paper

To Do

1. Have children use brushes to paint the palms of their hands (or the soles of their bare feet), then carefully press down on white paper or fabric squares to make prints.

2. When the paint is dry, ask children to write their names on their squares.

3. Have children work together to arrange their prints into a quilt.

Variations

◆ Have children lightly outline their hands on paper squares. Ask each child to write a sentence or two that describes an important personal quality or belief, following the outline of the hand. Children can sign and decorate the inside area of their handprints.

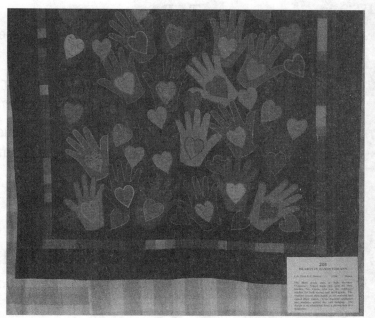

Collaborative class hand quilt

◆ Use a washable colored-ink pad to make fingerprints on the paper or fabric. Get some ideas from *Edward Emberley's Great Thumbprint Drawing Book* (Little, Brown, 1977) and use fine-tip markers to turn the fingerprints into whimsical people or animals.

 # Special Events Quilt

Here's a terrific way to chronicle a special event such as a field trip. These quilts also make great displays for Open School Night and wonderful prizes for a class raffle on the last day of school.

Materials

craft paper ◇ a variety of photos of children in action (or their own drawings about an event) ◇ paper and fabric scraps ◇ markers (or fabric markers) ◇ glue

To Do

1. Cut a large sheet of craft paper to the desired size of the finished quilt. Discuss placement of photos (or pictures) to show a progression of events.

2. Let children write captions for the photos on contrasting scraps using a fine-tip marker (select a fabric marker if children will be writing on cloth).

3. Using the crazy quilt technique of random overlapping, have children glue down photos and fabric or paper scraps until the entire surface of the craft paper is covered.

4. Laminate the quilt, if desired, for added durability.

 # Etch-a-Quilt

Children etch quilt designs into foam trays and use them to print quilt patterns.

Materials

foam meat trays ◇ ballpoint pens ◇ printing ink or tempera ◇ paintbrushes ◇ newsprint or craft paper

To Do

1. Demonstrate how to use a pointed object such as a ballpoint pen to etch a design into the back side of a foam tray. Have children then etch their own quilt designs on foam trays, using quilt resources as inspiration if desired.

2. To print the designs, have children brush a small amount of ink or paint over the entire surface of the design and firmly press the tray on the paper to make a relief, or reverse print, of the quilt pattern. Have children continue printing until the surface of the paper is decorated as desired.

TIP
Printed designs will be the mirror image of the foam tray etching plate. Letters should be written backward.

In conjunction with Etch-a-Quilt, share *Patchwork Tales* by Susan L. Roth and Ruth Phang, the story of a grandmother who shares with her granddaughter the family history behind the blocks in a patchwork quilt. Children will be intrigued by the illustrations, woodblock prints of the quilt blocks. Includes directions for making a quilt.

Adinkra *cloth quilt*

Adinkra Cloth

The Asante of Ghana are known for *adinkra,* or "good-bye" cloths, designed to celebrate the memory of departed loved ones. Worn on special occasions, *adinkra* cloths have meaningful symbols stamped in square pattern blocks. In the Asante tradition, children between the ages of 8 and 15 embroider and join together strips of cloth, then print the fabric using stamps made from broken gourds.

Materials
sponges ◇ scissors ◇ paint ◇ fabric squares or paper

To Do
Children can print their own *adinkra* cloths using sponges to stamp shapes. Have them draw designs on dry sponges and cut out the shapes (adult assistance recommended). When they are ready to print, have them dip the sponge stampers in paint and stamp on paper or fabric squares, then join them together to make a larger piece.

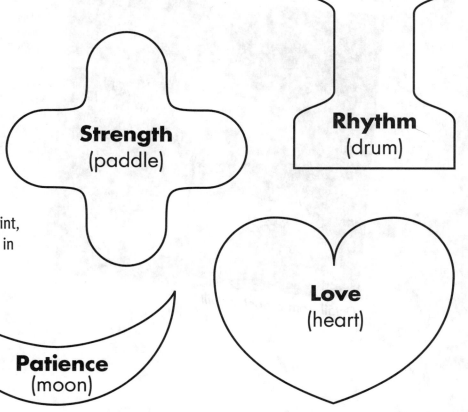

Strength
(paddle)

Rhythm
(drum)

Patience
(moon)

Love
(heart)

 Poetry Quilt

For a wonderful culminating poetry project, Patti Seifert's kindergarten class in Aspen, Colorado, creates poetry quilts. Here's a simplified version.

1. Ask children to paint pictures of the feelings or moods evoked by favorite poems. Have children use the same-size paper for their paintings, for example, 8-inch squares.

2. When paintings are dry, ask children to write their poems on the same paper.

3. Have children punch holes around the edges of their paintings, then take turns sewing the squares together with yarn to make a quilt. Display in your classroom quilt gallery and celebrate children's work!

Adapted from "A Poetry Quilt" by Patti Seifert, *Instructor* magazine, November/December 1994. By permission of *Instructor*.

Detail from a poetry quilt

A Culminating Quilt

From creating a prototype to tying the final knot, here's a step-by-step plan for making a paper or cloth quilt, along with suggestions for celebrating children's work at a traditional tying party.

Once children get caught up in the patterns, be prepared for them to begin clamoring to make their own fabric quilt! At this point, you'll need to decide how you want to proceed toward a final product. Your own quilting comfort level, availability of volunteers and materials, and the amount of time you want to devote to the project are all considerations, as are other goals you may have, such as the desire to use the quilt as a fund-raiser for a class or school trip or other special purpose.

ABC Quilts

If you are looking for a meaningful service project that can unify your class or even your whole school, consider making a crib quilt for babies who have AIDS. ABC (At-risk Babies Crib) Quilts is a nonprofit organization that supports volunteers in making and distributing these quilts. Children can involve the community by writing letters to local merchants soliciting quilting supplies and asking volunteers to lend a hand with cutting, piecing, and sewing. To learn more, share *Kids Making Quilts for Kids,* which has good directions for constructing soft but sturdy crib quilts that will stand up to lots of love and cuddling.

Student-Inspired Quilts

One of the beautiful things about quilting is that the ideas for patterns are often inspired by events of everyday life. Let that tradition continue to grow in your classroom as children decide on the artistic medium and patchwork method they'll use to create their quilt.

Here are some ideas that one of my first-grade classes suggested when I asked them for more ideas. I think they would have continued to brainstorm all day had I let them! Older children will certainly have some different ideas on their list.

- ◆ Family quilt
- ◆ Birthday quilt
- ◆ Postcard quilt
- ◆ Favorite Books quilt
- ◆ Earth Day quilt
- ◆ Greeting Card quilt
- ◆ Sports quilt
- ◆ Peace quilt
- ◆ Pets quilt

TIP

Authors generally receive mail through their publishers. Your school or public librarian can direct you to additional sources of author addresses. Be sure to include a self-addressed, postage-paid envelope for the author to return the quilt square.

 # Author Quilt

Karen Krupnick's fourth-grade students at Newman Elementary School in Chino, California, decided to remember all the wonderful books they read together by making a quilt of authors' signatures. They began by writing letters to favorite authors, including a quilt square with each. They explained the undertaking and requested that the author simply sign the quilt square. When the squares started coming back, children and classroom volunteers embroidered the signatures and joined the quilt blocks.

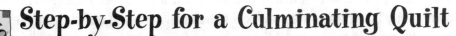 # Step-by-Step for a Culminating Quilt

Making a large quilt is indeed an undertaking but well worth the effort. The key is not to rush; six weeks is a conservative estimate of time if children can work on it a little bit every day. Wondering how to get started? First, organize some volunteers (parents, grandparents, and so on) who are willing to help out in various stages of the project. Then follow this suggested sequence of activities in which each child designs a block. Along the way, be sure to take plenty of pictures to share with children and their families—and use in a big book about your unit. (See Quilt-Tying Party, page 55.)

Step 1: Selecting Colors

It's tempting to set out all the construction paper colors you have so children will have many choices. However, if you plan on making a sewn quilt, that could mean translating 23 different paper colors into 23 different fabrics! To keep the color choices somewhat limited, you might have children look through books to find different color schemes and quilt patterns that are pleasing to them, then as a group select perhaps three or four light colors and three or four dark colors.

Step 2: Selecting Shapes

Stick to squares and triangles when making sewn quilts with young children. However, you may want to consider other geometric shapes such as hexagons, diamonds, and rectangles if you are making a nonsewn quilt.

Step 3: Selecting Sizes

Decide how big you want the finished quilt to be and calculate the block size based on the number of children in your class. (You can use the predetermined sizes provided here. See templates, pages 57–58.)

◆ **Block size:** A 7½-inch block (excluding seam allowances) works well (see template).

◆ **Pattern size:** For 7½-inch blocks, use 1½-inch paper squares. Cut triangles diagonally from the squares (see template). To simplify the process, you can use larger pattern pieces with the same size block. Paper squares that measure 2½ inches on each side will still let children have fun designing patterns and will be simpler to work with.

Step 4: Making a Prototype

Let children create prototypes of their designs, arranging construction paper shapes in the selected colors on quilt block–size squares (see Quilt Block template, page 57). Allow several sessions to make the prototypes. When children successfully combine squares and triangles, they will be very excited with their result! As children finalize their designs, they can paste them in place. If you are planning on making a fabric quilt, skip to Creating a Fabric Quilt (page 54). Otherwise, go to step 5 to learn how to piece together children's blocks.

Step 5: Joining Blocks and Rows

After children assemble their individual quilt blocks, it's time to talk about how to fit them all together. This is a fascinating process. Invite children to share their reasons for positioning different quilt squares, for example, to join patterns or colors that look good together, or to break up areas where there is too much of one color. What an exercise in consensus building and cooperative decision making! Talk about how it is difficult to see where each child's pattern starts and stops when they are close together. Then introduce the method of using strips to outline each quilt block. This is called a lattice, or interior border. Cut strips of paper (2 inches wide and as long as your finished squares) to make a lattice. Paste blocks in place on butcher paper then add a contrasting border to the quilt to complete the project.

Collaborative patchwork quilt

Creating a Fabric Quilt

If you want to turn children's paper prototypes into a fabric quilt, this is the time to organize volunteers. I set up a sewing area for a few weeks and let volunteers come in at any time of the day they can. (Schedule visits to avoid everyone coming at once.) An abbreviated outline of the process follows. Quilting books may also be helpful.

1. **Gather fabric.** One way to get the fabric you'll need is to send home construction paper color swatches and invite parents to send in scraps from home. Or ask for donations from local fabric stores. You may want to limit fabric selection to cottons. The actual print on the fabric is not important for sewing purposes, but the weight and fiber content are important if you will be stitching the quilt. If you are using fusible webbing to piece the quilt together, you can choose whatever fabrics you and children wish.

2. **Cut shapes.** Ask volunteers to cut out the fabric squares and triangles, using children's color and shape graph as a guide (see Great Graphing, page 55). Provide templates or dimensions (see page 58). If you are using fusible webbing for an iron-on quilt, you don't need to allow for seams. Just cut the shapes to actual size.

3. **Sort and stack.** Have children help sort fabric squares and triangles by color families and patterns. You might want to provide shoebox lids, containers, or trays for this.

4. **Piece it together.** Follow directions in a basic quilting book to piece the quilt together, adding a lattice and border. If you're making an iron-on quilt, just place the webbing between the shapes and the background fabric, and iron. Children can participate by using their paper patterns as a guide in laying out the fabric squares and triangles for the adult ironing volunteer.

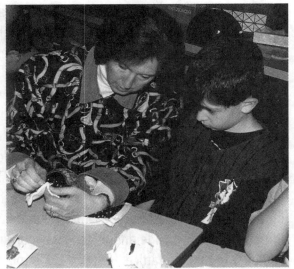

Working together to piece the quilt

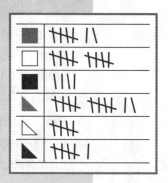

CULMINATING EXTENSION ACTIVITIES

Great Graphing

Whether children are creating a paper or fabric quilt, they'll have fun graphing by color and shape. Set up a graph as shown. Ask children to record how many squares and triangles of each color they used in their paper patterns by making tally marks in the appropriate rows.

    When everyone has had a chance to add to the graph, bring children together to total the tally marks. How many of each color and shape will they need to complete the quilt? Help children understand that graphing is a way quickly and accurately to gather this information.

■	ՊՊ l l
☐	ՊՊ ՊՊ
■	l l l l
◣	ՊՊ ՊՊ l l
◺	ՊՊ
◢	ՊՊ l

Textile Science

As an extension to your culminating quilting activities, invite children to view fabrics under a hand lens or microscope. Encourage children to describe what they see. Take time to discuss how the fabrics are alike and different in weave, color, and so on. Children might also like to play a matching game, drawing pictures of what different samples look like under a microscope and challenging one another to match the drawings to the actual fabric samples.

 ## Quilt-Tying Party

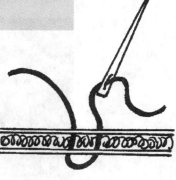

A quick way to sandwich together the layers of a quilt is to tie the quilt with simple knots, using embroidery floss (see illustration). After learning about the quilting bees of days gone by, my first graders like to have their own version of a quilting party. It's a festive way to wrap up the unit and to share children's work with their families. Let children help you plan the party. If you'll actually be tying a fabric quilt, you may want to get a head start and finish it at the party. (Check a quilter's book for directions on putting the backing, batting, and quilt top together and tying the knots.) Here are suggested activities for the event.

◆ **Make invitations.** Have children use what they have learned about quilt patterns to create quilt-tying party invitations. It's fun to do this by hand or with computer software (see Resources, page 62).

◆ **Sign the quilt.** As guests look on, let children take turns signing their names to the quilt. Be sure to record the date and place, too. Who knows where your quilt might travel in its lifetime and who might inherit it? Whatever its future, everyone will know its history! (Use a permanent marker or embroidery thread for a fabric quilt.)

◆ **Make a big book.** Just as important as making the actual quilt squares and the quilt itself is having children look back at their quilting experience. By now, you've probably amassed lots of photographs of children in action, as well as samples of their written and patterning work. Let everyone help assemble and mount these for a class big book. Try to include some of children's paper prototypes, a photo of the finished quilt, and a chart showing which child made which block.

◆ **Play quilting games.** Make a few extra copies of Quilt Match (page 14) so that several groups of children and adults can play. Challenge your guests' memories, too, by playing a round of Quilts in the Attic (page 12).

◆ **Play quilting music.** *The Heart of Quilting* will add an authentic touch to your quilt-tying party.

Above all, enjoy the sense of togetherness and spirit of cooperation that emanate from your quilting project. You and your class have worked to create a beautiful, meaningful treasure!

Students explore a quilt at a local museum

Quilt Block Template

Shape Templates

**Cut on the dotted lines for a paper quilt.
Cut on solid lines for a fabric quilt (to
allow for a ¼-inch seam allowance).**

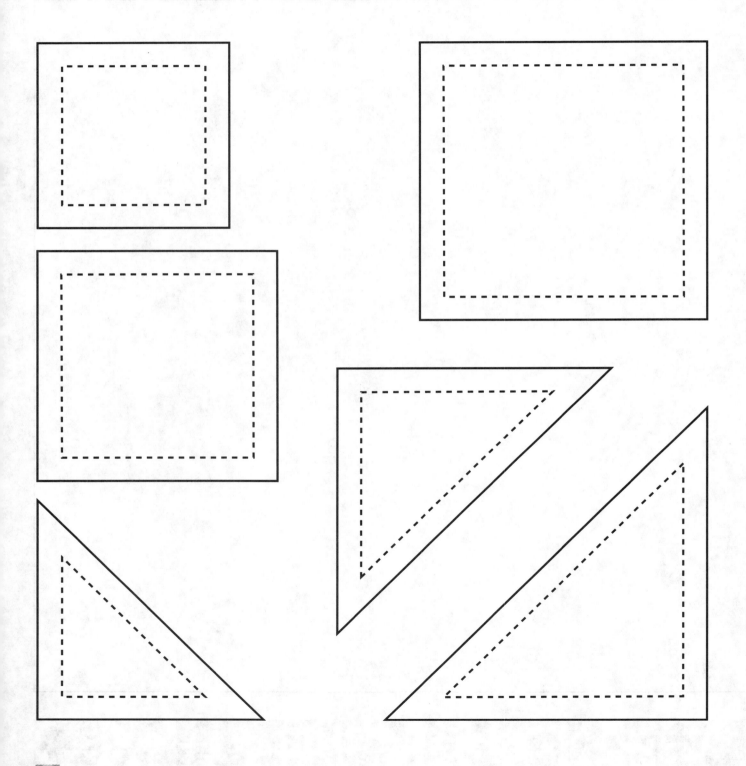

Resources

For Children

These wonderful picture books are great for whole-class read-alouds or for children to enjoy on their own.

A Cloak for the Dreamer by Aileen Friedman (Scholastic, 1994). Three sons of a tailor each try to sew a patchwork cloak for the king. One son learns a lot about shapes—and himself—in the process.

Aunt Harriet and the Underground Railroad in the Sky by Faith Ringgold (Crown, 1992). Using the story quilt technique, Ringgold tells the story of young Cassie retracing Underground Railroad routes—with Harriet Tubman as her guide.

Eight Hands Round by Ann Whitford Paul (HarperCollins, 1991). Illustrates 26 different quilt patterns from *A* to *Z*.

Faith Ringgold by Robyn Montana Turner (Little, Brown, 1993). A biography of the author, story quilter, and artist.

The Gingham Dog and the Calico Cat by Eugene Field (Philomel, 1990). Two stuffed animals lose control in an antique shop in the middle of the night.

The Josefina Story Quilt by Eleanor Coerr (HarperCollins, 1986). The experiences of a pioneer family traveling west in the 1850s are stitched into a young girl's first quilt.

The Keeping Quilt by Patricia Polacco (Simon and Schuster, 1988). A poignant and meaningful story that shows how quilts tie families together across generations.

Kids Making Quilts for Kids by ABC Quilts (The Quilt Press, 1994). A guide to making quilts for babies who are in the hospital with AIDS.

My Grandmother's Patchwork Quilt by Janet Bolton (Delacorte, 1993). A grandmother's narrative of her childhood, as piece by piece, memory by memory, a quilt takes shape. Includes instructions for re-creating Grandmother's quilt.

Patchwork Island by Karla Kuskin (HarperCollins, 1994). A young mother makes a quilt for her baby that captures the essence of the special island where they live.

The Patchwork Quilt by Valerie Flournoy (Dial, 1985). This story follows a grandmother and granddaughter as they work on a family patchwork quilt. A good introduction to the multigenerational bridge quilts can provide.

Patchwork Tales by Susan L. Roth and Ruth Phang (Atheneum, 1984). A grandmother shares with her granddaughter the family history behind the blocks in a patchwork quilt. Illustrated with woodblock prints of the quilt blocks. Includes directions for making a quilt.

Q Is for Quilt: An ABC Quilt Pattern Book by Gwen Marston (Michigan State University Museum, 1987). Simple text and illustrations are perfect for replicating patterns with math manipulatives.

The Quilt Story by Tony Johnston (Putnam, 1985). This simple story demonstrates how quilts have memories and lives all their own.

The Rag Coat by Lauren Mills (Little, Brown, 1991). A beautiful story that shows how every scrap of fabric is needed and used to make a quilted patchwork coat for a young girl. Acceptance and tolerance of others is the underlying message of the story.

Sam Johnson and the Blue Ribbon Quilt by Lisa Campbell Ernst (Lothrop, 1983). A memorable story that shows many quilt patterns, celebrates originality and resourcefulness, and illustrates how men can quilt as well as women. A favorite with children.

Stitching Stars: The Story Quilts of Harriet Powers by Mary Lyons (Scribners, 1993). A fascinating illustrated biography of a former Georgia slave girl and the story quilts she made.

Sweet Clara and the Freedom Quilt by Deborah Hopkinson (Knopf, 1993). An inspiring story about a young slave girl who learns to quilt, and a special quilt she creates that serves as a road map to freedom for many others.

Tar Beach by Faith Ringgold (Crown, 1991). Each page shows a segment of a story quilt about the author's childhood.

For Teachers

You'll find lots of color and black and white illustrations in these books that children can use as inspiration for their own patterning work.

Encyclopedia of Pieced Quilt Patterns compiled by Barbara Brackman (American Quilting Society, 1993). A compendium of hundreds of patterns, shown in black and white thumbnail sketches.

Lap Quilting with George Bonesteel by Georgia Bonesteel (Oxmoor House, 1990). Terrific grayscale diagrams make great models for children to replicate with manipulatives.

Patchwork Math 1 and *Patchwork Math 2* by Debra Baycura (Scholastic, 1990). Students of all ages are sure to love these unique math activity pages.

Quilting Patterns from Native American Designs by Joyce Mari (American Quilting Society, 1993). An excellent reference for studying symmetry and design.

Quilts: An American Heritage by Terri Zegart (Smithmark, 1994). Bursting with more than 130 color photographs and on sale at mall bookstores at drastically less than the retail price.

Quilts: From Colonial to Contemporary by Lucy Folmar Bullard (Publications International, 1992). Full-color photos are simply sumptuous. Check sale sections at local booksellers.

Star Quilt Designs by Doreen L. Saunders (Dover, 1991). A wonderful reference for patterning and symmetry ideas.

Treasury of Patchwork Quilt Sets by Elizabeth F. Nyhan (Dover, 1994). The many line drawings are perfect for reproducing and coloring.

Software

Children can employ some of the same techniques as quilters who use software to experiment with pattern and design.

KidPix (Broderbund, 800-521-6263). An ideal introduction to computer-assisted quilt design. Children can draw square outlines for quilt blocks, adding lines and diagonals to create patches, then filling in patches with pattern and paint tools, built-in stampers, or freehand designs. They can use the stampers to create calico designs for quilting projects, too.

***PCQuilt*/BabyMac** (Nina Antze, 707-823-8494). Design and color quilt blocks, and with a click of the mouse multiply those blocks into a picture of a full quilt.

Quilting Bee (MECC, 800-685-MECC). Choose from 12 geometric shapes to design quilt squares in many colors.

Audiovisual

The Magic Quilt (National Film Board of Canada, Pacific Productions, 1985). In this video, the importance of cooperation and team spirit is portrayed when a group of children discover a magic quilt on a rainy summer day.

The Heart of Quilting: Stories and Songs Celebrating Quilting Legend and Lore by Dan Duggan and Cathy Barbano (Esperance Music Productions, 315-754-8946). Soothing dulcimer music with poetry and quilters' anecdotes.

NOTES

Author's Bio

Wendy Buchberg is a producer at Scholastic Network, where she develops innovative cross-curricular telecommunications projects on the World Wide Web. She has written articles for *Instructor* and *Technology Connection* magazines, drawing from her 23 years of experience teaching grades pre-K through 12 in upstate New York public schools. As a longtime admirer of American quilts, she began incorporating quilting as a teaching theme in her elementary school classes and found her students and their families as motivated as she was to combine the art and inspiration of quilting into everyday school subjects such as reading, social studies, science, math, and writing.

Wendy lives in Ithaca, New York, with her husband and two daughters.